SNACKS
THOUGHT

SNACKS FOR THOUGHT

SELF REMINDER

samson yung-Abu

ISBN: Softcover   978-1-6641-1231-5
               eBook   978-1-6641-1230-8

Print information available on the last page.

Rev. date: 08/12/2020

To order additional copies of this book, contact:
Xlibris
UK TFN: 0800 0148620 (Toll Free inside the UK)
UK Local: 02036 956328 (+44 20 3695 6328 from outside the UK)
www.Xlibrispublishing.co.uk
Orders@Xlibrispublishing.co.uk
818303

*When life gives you darkness, paint stars
on it and make a beautiful sky*

Introduction

*"A successful day starts with a plan to have
one. Have a happy Smiley day."*

My aim is to tell you things you already know, in ways you never knew, with inspirational messages to promote wiser, healthier living. I see myself not just as a writer, but also as an artist who paints with words - one who uses a blank page as a canvas, to paint the world a little brighter.

We shouldn't need many words to make sense of life. Motivation is, in my view, a simple explanation of the chaos we live in. The world as we know it, in our brief existence so far, can be toxic. If we let ourselves, we will often feel negative before we even step out the door. So when you get up in the morning, the first words you read should be optimistic and uplifting. This act reflects the value of your mental health, your appreciation of your natural grace and your desire to feel better all day long.

I AM
Strong

even your DARKNESS has STARS

Many people hide away from their troubles. The truth is that when you face your problems, you often encounter your stronger self. If you address your darkness, you will see the light that shines in the midst of it.

I AM

Brilliant

DON'T be blind to YOUR BLESSINGS

You are amazing and suited for greatness. Don't let anyone tell you otherwise, not even you. Making do with less is to sabotage your own happiness. If life wasn't that bad, we wouldn't be wishing for greater things. It is therefore very important to open your eyes. To know when to walk away and when to move on.

I AM

Wise

be supportive, BUT not at your own expense

To be happy yourself, you must support others and share their happiness. But watch your reputation - some people will rely on you, even if they can help themselves. Constantly worrying about the same people can make you part of the problem. You are their solution, so they don't mind creating more problems. And you start solving their problems at the expense of your own.

I AM

CONFIDENT

SELF-ACCEPTANCE means growth

Resenting any part of ourselves is to reject our uniqueness. To accept yourself takes inner strength and courage. When you truly recognise yourself, it is a new sensation. Some of us are so far from self-discovery that we never truly connect with anyone, even the people that seem to care. You must represent yourself as you are.

I AM

A FIGHTER

resist WHEN YOUR AUDIENCE LAUGH AT YOUR FALL

Sometimes we avoid taking risks because we know
people will gloat if we fail. But those same people
will applaud themselves if you don't take any chances
at all. Let them talk, laugh, or whatever else they
feel might crush your courage. Don't entertain
it with mindless attention. Do what you need to
do. That is your focus and your distraction.

I AM

INTREPID

IT ALL DEPENDS ON YOU!

Your dream depends on the direction you take.
Your direction depends on the decisions you make.
Your dedication leads to your destination.

I AM

A GOAL-GETTER

HARD WORK brings
OPPORTUNITIES on the way

Each day you work hard, you drive yourself closer to your goal. The best part is that on your way, you find unexpected opportunities. By the time you succeed, you will have made new and better friends and gained more experience, more exposure and more options to pursue.

I AM

HEALTHY

IF YOU FORCE LOVE, it won't succeed

If we yearn for a lost love, we only torture ourselves. The heart is intelligent. It knows what it wants, but it also knows what it cannot have. Often, we ignore our intuition and try to fight for what is already lost. Move on! A good heart can always heal, as long as it isn't holding on to the past.

I AM

TALENTED

YOUR value is YOUR MIND, NOT YOUR MONEY

Being rich does not increase your value, but your value gives you the opportunity to acquire wealth. But it doesn't stop there – value also gives you the respect of others.

I AM

ENOUGH

YOU ARE DOING A GREAT JOB ON YOURSELF

It takes a lot to be enough. Doing what you can is all you need to do. You are doing a great job! Keep going – that's enough.

I AM

READY

TAKE EVERY OPPORTUNITY you can

Opportunities sometimes lead to more wishes.
And if we yearn for something, we could be
blessed with a chance that is not exactly what
we wished for. But take every opportunity!

I AM

INVOLVED

GET A GRIP ON YOUR WHEELS

Stop sitting in the passenger seat of your own Rolls-Royce. Seize the steering wheel of your day: we are going my way, from now on. No ifs, no buts, no exceptions, no excuses.

I AM

Active

IF YOU THINK ALL DAY, YOU WILL WORRY ALL NIGHT

Some of us never get anything done, never achieve anything big or never become anyone of value. All we do is worry, overthinking everything. Get something done!

I AM

Decisive

LETTING GO ISN'T QUITTING

Don't let anyone call you a quitter for letting
go. Some people will push it too far, push you
too far and you realise they never respected your
boundaries. At that point, you should know it is a
wise decision and wonderful timing to let go.

I AM

COMMITTED

IF YOU CAN'T be MOTIVATed, be DISCIPLINEd

You gotta do what you gotta do, even when all you wanna do is none of it. Sometimes we wake up and we don't feel motivated, no matter how hard we try. At this point, we must apply absolute discipline and mental strength. Push yourself to get up and get on with it - whether you want to, or not.

I AM

Over it

WINNERS are VICTORs, NOT VICTIms

The lingering pain doesn't mean the battle wasn't
won. But, some of us choose to remain stuck in a
place of vulnerability. We refuse every opportunity
to let go and forget. Dwelling on the pain of the
past hurts healing scars. Learn to move on.

I AM

Uɴɪϙᴜᴇ

YOUR SELF IS THE BEST
THING ABOUT YOU

When you pretend to be someone else in
order to be accepted, you automatically reject
yourself – by pretending that you don't exist. That
is the highest form of betrayal to oneself.

I AM

RESOURCEFUL

Use your time WISEly

Be resourceful with your efforts and take your opportunities reliably. If you have time to play, you have time to plan. If you have time for struggles, you have time for solutions. If you have time for problems, you have time for peace.

I AM

ALL-IN

YOU CAN't do your half-best and expeCt full success

For the progress you desire, you must take the actions needed – to the best of your ability. Some people fail because they are not completely invested in their future. Expecting great results from average efforts is like trying to buy an item in a grocery store with half a bank note. Day in, day out, you must be fully committed to get what you want.

I AM

Daring

Listen to your hunger – it reveals
YOUR AMBITIONS

Dare your intuition and put it to the test – see how
far you can go in your success. Some people act like
experts in your field, and yet they fail to get past
the most basic of challenges in their own life.

I AM

BOLD

Break free from THE opinions OF OTHERS

Often, people are scared of who you could become. They tell you it is impossible to be free. They control your movement, so they can have power. They contain your strength, so they don't expose their weakness. They limit your happiness, so they can deny their sadness. They blame you for your pain, so they don't face their guilt.

I AM

O PEN-MINDED

if you are stuck, try a different perspective

Be open to something new. One of the best ways to grow and achieve is to connect with others, and learn from them. This presents you with more options to solve those tough and important problems, that you might lack the experience to address yourself.

I AM

SERENE

ignore negativity

Most of the time, happiness cannot last because negative people have unlimited access to our heart. We make ourselves available to pessimism and sadness. We are so exposed that they enter our lives whenever they want, cause damage and leave as quickly, and as easily, as they came in.

I AM

Sure

know that you are amazing

What you say about yourself is more powerful than
the words of others. You are not useless, ugly, pathetic,
or a freak. You are authentic, powerful, priceless,
and sexy. Tell yourself, and let everyone know it.

I AM

Wonderful

Own your greatness, and build your best

You are blessed with thought, because life has challenges waiting for you. You have a talent, so use it. With your wonderful, intelligent brain, you must learn to become more. Become strong, not stressed. Deal with your mess, instead of being overcome by it.

I AM

A LEARNER

permit yourself to try

Take a chance and try something new. Sometimes we are scared and play the 'safe card' by not attempting anything, hiding from new opportunities. The truth is, you won't get it right all the time. But things will always work out, if you do what you believe is right. Opportunity is only available if you have the freedom to fail. Only those who try can flourish.

I AM

INSPIRED

if you are motivated, mountains are stairs

Most people quit when the path ahead looks tougher than they thought. They see only impossibility, where they should see challenges. They see themselves too small and too weak. They have no idea that the peak is surmountable, if only they apply that extra motivation.

I AM

ACCOUNTABLE

Establish your happiness within

You alone own your happiness. Never depend on anyone else for your wellbeing. If you rely on someone who can't make you happy, it means they cannot be happy themselves. If they are not happy, they have no spare feelings for you.

I AM

WINNING

be a winner, not a whiner

Wake up daily and see yourself as a success. You have made it to today, and that is a victory. Don't envy anyone: we all have problems that go beyond our appearances. Everyone is fighting to keep it together: to feel okay, to laugh, to love and be loved, to lead. The intensity of your problems is no less, and theirs is no greater than ours. Be supportive, be kind, be helpful, be you.

I AM

IMPORTANT

YOU ARE JUDGED on
your own self-worth

You must see your own importance before anyone will respect you. Most people will belittle themselves until they can be used as others see fit. But know this: your self-projection will be accepted. If you take yourself seriously enough, others will do the same.

I AM

Humble

the right attitude gets on with life

With the help of good manners, kindness often brings new opportunities. In order to be successful and happy, you must manage your blessings with humbleness. If not, all of your good fortune could vanish, leaving you cold and alone.

I AM

NICE-LOOKING

Looking good starts with liking your body

You are unique and that itself is good enough.
Most people look to others as a mirror, and when
the bodies don't match, they feel inferior. But
feeling attractive starts when you physically accept
yourself – in comparison to no one else. Embrace
yourself – you are awesome just the way you are.

I AM

GIVING

Givers receive generosity

Many people want more, without giving themselves.
So they run dry in their resources. The truth is
that one good seed can produce great results. But
more importantly, you have to plant many seeds
for a fruitful tree. So give generously. Do this, and
you will get more than you could ever want.

I AM

INVENTIVE

use ingenuity to find your way

Life is like a giant maze with a guiding light that flickers bright, or vanishes. We are constantly having to survive until we can hope again. The truth is that clever people do well in life because they adapt to changes. Creativity is a primitive skill, part of our survival kit. And the good news is, we all have it. From birth, it has helped us to thrive in storms, summon our strength and overcome our obstacles.

I AM

LUCKY

LUCK comes to those who try

Some of us constantly feel unlucky, and believe that fortune is never on our side. But could it be that we are idle and distracted? The truth is that to be lucky, there needs to be something for luck to act on. This will get you the opportunity you wish for.

I AM

Oɴ ᴛᴏᴘ

VISUALISE your success

Imagine you are on top of your problems – this puts
you in a powerful place. Our vision eventually becomes
our version of reality, as we become what we think.
A stuck imagination limits your vision of where you
can go. Keep your eyes above the mountain and
pretty soon, the bottom will be a distant memory.

I AM

Valiant

Bravery should be humble

The world demands that we are tough and fearless in the face of difficulty. To achieve greatness, we must be valiant. It is not enough to be smart, attractive or educated. You must develop a bravado that captivates others, but in the most humble way.

I AM

EFFORTFUL

effort gets you further, but courage gets you through

To achieve anything, you must put in the effort. Nothing is truly valuable unless you have worked hard to earn it. But don't forget courage. It will get you past the finishing line when quitting starts playing on your mind.

I AM

Mɪɴᴅꜰᴜʟ

kindness is on the tip of your tongue: THINK first

Words are the very important choice of what to say and how to say it. Yes, we often want to speak our minds. But, for the sake of your success and peace of mind, you must pause. You must think before you speak – we cannot take back the words we utter in haste. We must ask ourselves: is our desire for expression kind? If so, say what you want, in the most suitable way.

I AM

EXCEPTIONAL

TO THINK ANY LESS OF
YOURSELF IS DEGRADING

There is nothing baser in life than believing you are
as less than sacred. Even animals don't think badly of
themselves. We are born great and we owe it to ourselves
to feel great, think great, act great, and become great.

Letter To self

DEAR ME,

I AM A FIGHTER. I AM COURAGEOUS.
I AM A WINNER. I LOVE ME.

HAVE A GREAT DAY!

Lightning Source UK Ltd.
Milton Keynes UK
UKHW011109060223
416538UK00001B/143